Stevie's New Friend

Kathryn Ulberg Lilleby

Illustrations by Chad Chronick

Oncology Nursing Press, Inc.

Publisher: Leonard Mafrica, MBA, CAE
Technical Publications Editor: Barbara Sigler, RN, MNEd
Staff Editors: Lisa M. George, BA, Jennifer Krause, BA
Creative Services Assistants: Chad Chronick, Dany Sjoen

Stevie's New Blood

Library of Congress Catalog Card Number: 00-102213

ISBN 1-890504-17-3

Publisher's Note

This book is published by the Oncology Nursing Press, Inc. (ONP). ONP neither represents nor guarantees that the practices described herein will, if followed, ensure safe and effective patient care. The recommendations contained in this book reflect ONP's judgment regarding the state of general knowledge and practice in the field as of the date of publication. The recommendations may not be appropriate for use in all circumstances. Those who use this book should make their own determinations regarding specific safe and appropriate patient-care practices, taking into account the personnel, equipment, and practices available at the hospital or other facility at which they are located. The author and publisher cannot be held responsible for any liability incurred as a consequence of the use or application of any of the contents of this book. Mention of specific products and opinions related to those products do not indicate or imply endorsement by ONS or ONP.

ONS and ONP publications are originally published in English. Permission has been granted by the ONS Board of Directors for foreign translation. (Individual tables and figures that are reprinted or adapted require additional permission from the original source.) However, because translations from English may not always be accurate and precise, ONS and ONP disclaim any responsibility for inaccurate translations. Readers relying on precise information should check the original English version.

Printed in the United States of America

Oncology Nursing Press, Inc.
A subsidiary of the Oncology Nursing Society

This book is dedicated to Stephen Paul Lowry (1958~1961), who died from leukemia before the advent of bone marrow transplantation.

Acknowledgements

My heartfelt thanks go to Teri Hein, a teacher at the Hutch School, and Lisa Lange and Alison Cushing, child life specialists at Swedish Hospital Medical Center, for their collaboration in the formation of this book. My thanks also to the patients, siblings, and parents at Fred Hutchinson Cancer Research Center for contributing their honest and candid comments about their experiences. Fred Appelbaum, MD, director of the Clinical Division at Fred Hutchinson Cancer Research Center, receives my thanks for his encouragement and counsel. And much appreciation goes to Barbara Sigler, technical publications editor, and Chad Chronick, illustrator, of the Oncology Nursing Press, because they love Stevie as much as I do.

Introduction

This book tells the story of Stevie, who is undergoing bone marrow transplant (BMT) in the hopes that it will cure his leukemia. Anna, his sister—and donor—will learn what it is like to give her bone marrow. The story explains BMT from a child's point of view and can be adapted for children of various ages. The pictures illustrate the story for younger children who cannot yet read, and children from the ages of 6~10 can read the easily understood, large-print words. Smaller print on opposing pages provides older children and parents with more detailed information. The book also can be adapted for the child whose parent is having a transplant or for the friend of a child undergoing BMT.

The process of producing blood is called hematopoiesis. Blood starts out as a stem cell—the parent cell of all types of blood cells. It then becomes either a lymphoid stem cell or a myeloid stem cell. Lymphoid stem cells become either T cells or B cells. Myeloid stem cells can become red blood cells, platelets, or a type of white cell. Each cell has specific duties. Red blood cells carry oxygen to the tissues of the body, and platelets help blood to clot when a blood vessel is cut. White cells come in several types and have a variety of responsibilities. Granulocytes and monocytes help to fight infections, and lymphocytes regulate the immune system. The body also makes special proteins called growth factors that stimulate the stem cells, thereby determining which type of cells they will become and then multiplying that kind of cell and maturing the cells to ensure that they will do their job correctly and efficiently.

E veryone has a factory inside his or her bones that makes blood. Blood has red cells, white cells, and platelets. Red blood cells carry oxygen to all parts of our body. White blood cells fight germs, and platelets plug up cuts so that they stop bleeding.

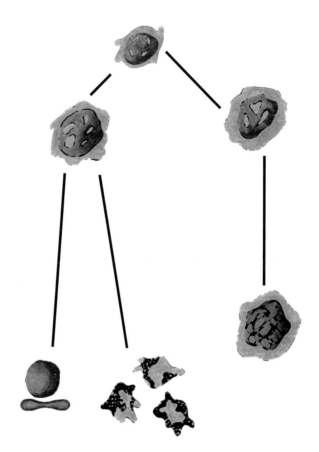

Leukemia is called cancer of the blood because the bone marrow makes too many white cells. Immature white blood cells called blasts multiply uncontrollably and pack the long, narrow shafts of bone with leukemic cells so that good red blood cells and platelets are crowded out. Signs and symptoms of leukemia include fatigue or paleness of the skin because the red blood count (hemoglobin or hematocrit) is low and not enough oxygen is getting to the body. In addition, bruises or nose bleeds might occur easily because the platelet count is low.

Cancer is any uncontrolled growth of cells. When a lump of malignant (cancer) cells develops, it is called a tumor. The cause of cancer is generally unknown, but some cancers seem to be common in families or due to environmental factors. Cancer is not contagious, and it's no one's fault when it develops.

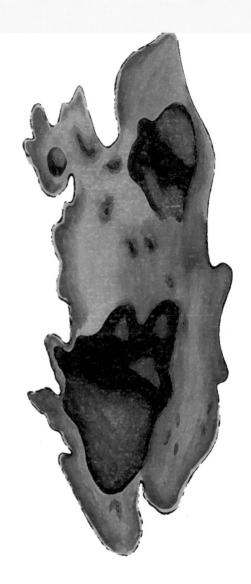

S ometimes the factory doesn't work right and makes too many white blood cells. That's what happened to Stevie. The white blood cells took up all the room in his bones, and the red blood cells and the platelets didn't have enough space. This is called leukemia or cancer of the blood. It wasn't Stevie's fault that he got leukemia, and it's not catchy like a cold.

Many cancers can be treated successfully with chemotherapy or radiation therapy. Chemotherapy uses medicines to actually kill the malignant cells by stopping their ability to grow. Radiation works in a similar way but is given by machines. However, each has the side effect of damaging healthy tissue while destroying the malignant cells. Doses of chemotherapy and radiation are carefully prescribed so that enough is administered to kill the cancer but not all of the normal cells. One of the most severe side effects of these treatments is damage to the bone marrow, where blood is formed. Patients cannot survive if their bone marrow doesn't make blood cells.

If the cancer comes back after treatment, it is called "relapse," and more chemotherapy or radiation is needed. After many years of study, doctors know when it is unlikely that the cancer can be treated with chemotherapy at the regular doses and when a bone marrow transplant (BMT) is needed.

BMT takes place after high-dose chemotherapy and/or radiation therapy to counteract, or rescue the patient from, the side effects of these treatments. A dose of chemotherapy high enough to kill the cancer also kills good bone marrow cells, leaving them unable to produce blood. Therefore, new bone marrow must come from a healthy donor or from bone marrow the patient stored while in remission. If a patient doesn't receive healthy bone marrow after high-dose chemotherapy, he could die from infection or bleeding because of low white blood cell or platelet counts.

S tevie already had chemotherapy to get rid of the bad cells, but the leukemia came back. Now his doctor says BMT might be best. BMT makes the factory work right again. The bad cells are killed, and the new, healthy cells make the factory start making good blood again.

BMT centers are all over the United States and in many countries around the world, but there may not be one near everyone's home. Moving to a different city is complicated, and deciding whether the whole family should move can be difficult. Here are some comments from people who experienced the move.

"I think it is very important for the whole family to go through this together. There are times when you need to lean on each other for support." Kristine, age 16

"It was difficult during the time my husband and our other child had to fly back home when he had to go to work. The times we were together made life seem more normal, not so isolated. My husband said that if it had to be done again, the family would not be separated." Jennifer, mother of BMT recipient

"We almost stayed home, but I was so glad we went because the patient really needs family there. You also get to meet many new people and stay in a wonderful city." Elisabeth, age 15, daughter of BMT recipient

"My older brother had to stay home. He stayed out of trouble and made the honor roll at school. This made things easier for my mom because she didn't have to worry about him doing something stupid, and I didn't have to worry about him as much." Ethel, age 15

O nly special hospitals have BMT units, so Stevie and his family moved to a different city. He had to say good-bye to his friends for a while. His brother, Christopher, stayed home with his aunt and uncle so he could finish the school year, and Stevie left his favorite toy with him. They promised to send pictures and letters and to talk on the phone.

Stevie took some special things besides what his Mom packed for him—favorite books, videos, and pictures of his family, friends, and Molly, his golden retriever. His stuffed teddy, Bear, will keep him company when he feels sick or scared.

Arriving at the BMT unit can be overwhelming. New doctors, nurses, technicians, support staff, and routines can cause stress. This is the time to ask lots of questions and read all the information. Nurses, social workers, chaplains, and other families can provide a lot of support. Feeling isolated and scared isn't uncommon.

The patient and family will be busy with clinic visits, tests, conferences, and consent forms. With the transplant, a chance for hope and a cure is in sight.

A randomized study is when half of the patients are given a certain drug and the other half are given the standard treatment or a placebo. This is the only scientific way of proving that the new treatment is better than the standard treatment.

Deciding to sign an informed-consent form can be difficult. The doctor talks about the reason for the study, the risks and benefits of participating in the study, and alternative treatments. Informed-consent forms help to explain the reason for certain treatments and why they may help the patient.

The tests that are done when you arrive at the BMT unit are necessary to evaluate the best treatment for the patient. They also will be used to help to analyze whether the patient had the best response to that treatment after transplant. Future patients will benefit from what the doctors have learned as a result of treating many patients with the same disease in the same way.

This is how some patients felt when they got to the BMT unit.

"When I got to the BMT unit, I didn't know anything about transplant. I wanted to know what kinds of things they were going to do to me and how many shots I'd have to have." Jarrett, age 5

"Before, when I didn't know much about transplant, I was scared about the process. Then, after my doctor explained it to me, I was more at ease with the thought of going through the transplant." Tamisha, age 18

When Stevie got to the new hospital, many things needed to be done. Stevie, Anna, and their parents met their new doctors and nurses. They learned their way from their apartment to the hospital and explored the new city, with its parks and stores. Mostly, however, Stevie had lots of appointments.

The doctors needed to know all about his leukemia so that they could give him the best chemotherapy and radiation treatment. Stevie's mom and dad signed lots of papers, giving the doctors permission to take care of Stevie in the best way. At the same time, the doctors were learning more about cancer and how to cure it so that other people could get better, too.

In order to gain central venous access, a semipermanent IV silicone tube is inserted into the large subclavian vein (under the collar bone), which goes into the top chamber of the heart called the right atrium. The end of the tube is tunneled under the skin so that it comes out of the upper chest. A Dacron cuff and a suture secure it there. Some common central venous access devices are Hickman catheter, Groshong catheter, or central line. Central venous access devices are inserted in the operating room with the patient under anesthesia.

A central line is used to draw blood samples and administer medications, IV fluids, and blood products. It eliminates the need for healthcare providers to continually use a needle for these procedures. A central line requires careful, sterile care so that it doesn't become infected or pulled out. The nurse teaches parents and older siblings how to clean the skin and change the dressing around the line.

How do patients feel about their catheter?

"Having a Hickman line in was very helpful during my transplant and immediately afterwards. I had so many blood draws and infusions that it was good not having to be poked all the time." David, age 11

"I remember going to sleep and waking up to the Hickman catheter hurting sometimes." Anna, age 8

"Getting the Hickman catheter was a little scary for me, but one of the technicians came out and explained the process of how it would go into my chest." Tamisha, age 18

S tevie didn't have a central line, so a doctor put one in his chest in the operating room. He was a little scared, but his mom and dad and the nurse told him all about it. He was asleep, so the procedure didn't hurt. Having a central line was great because he didn't get any more pokes! The nurse took all the blood tests from it and gave all his medicines, blood transfusions, and IVs through it.

The side effects of chemotherapy and radiation are caused by the damage they do to healthy cells. Any type of cell that normally divides rapidly, such as hair cells, skin cells, and the cells in the lining of the mouth, stomach, intestines, liver, kidneys, and lungs, is affected. The patient may experience hair loss. In addition, nausea, vomiting, and diarrhea are common, and kidney and liver function may decrease.

These side effects are usually temporary and reversible. The nurse will administer medications to control the nausea, vomiting, and diarrhea, and the hair eventually will grow back.

"When my hair started to grow back, it came in more straight, but as time went on, my hair turned to loose curls—before I had really tight curly hair. The color came back the same." Tamisha, age 18

"My dad's hair was blonde, like mine. It grew back thinner, grayer, and he didn't get much back! Just enough to cover his head and little more. When we returned from the hospital, all the kids thought my Dad was in the army because he was bald!" Emily, age 8, daughter of BMT recipient

"All of my hair grew back except for two circles on top of my head, where I had extra radiation. They told me that it probably won't come back in those spots. I'm thinking about getting a hairpiece just so I don't have to answer so many questions." Jarrett, age 5

W hen it was time to kill the leukemia in Stevie's blood, the doctor told him that chemotherapy was the strongest medicine he would get.

"It will make you sick, Stevie," he said. "You'll feel sick to your stomach and throw up. You'll probably have to go to the bathroom a lot. But the nurses will give you medicine to help you feel better."

Stevie's hair started falling out. It was kind of hard to get used to, but the nurse said, "Just when you're getting used to it, guess what? It starts growing back in!"

Total body irradiation has two purposes. One is to kill all cancer cells in the body. The other is to destroy the bone marrow to make room for the new transplanted bone marrow to grow.

A specially trained x-ray technician measures the patient to ensure that the right dose of radiation is prescribed. Some days, the patient lies on his back, and others, on his side. Sometimes, the radiation is given once a day. Other times, the shorter, more frequent doses are given two or three times daily.

What were the three scariest things during the transplant?

"Pulling the catheter, some of my friends dying, and not knowing what radiation would be like." Tyler, age 8

"I was scared my Hickman might come loose or my little sister might pull on it. Other than that, I wasn't scared of anything." Jarrett, age 5

"Being really weak, and I didn't know if I would walk again, the pain in my mouth, and going through the transplant." Cynthia, age 12

A nother way to kill the bad cells is with strong x-rays. Stevie was taken to a special room with a bed between two x-ray machines. He was alone in the room while he got the radiation, but the nurse could hear him talk and could see him. It didn't hurt, and he couldn't feel anything. Afterwards, he felt tired and a little sick to his stomach, but the nurse gave him medicine to help him feel better.

Stem cells are found in several places in the body. They are found in the bone marrow, in the blood circulating through the body, and in the blood that is left in the umbilical cord and placenta after a baby is born.

Bone marrow is "harvested" from the donor in the operating room with the patient under general anesthesia. The doctors insert a large needle into the hip bones in the back and suction out the bone marrow a tablespoonful at a time. Because the bone marrow is a spongy material with compartments like a honeycomb, the needle is inserted at a slightly different angle each time so that more marrow can be pulled out. This is repeated about a hundred times to get about a quart of bone marrow for an adult or four tablespoonfuls for every pound of weight in a child. After the donor wakes up, he may have pain in his hips for a day or so, but otherwise, there are no serious side effects.

Peripheral blood stem cells (PBSC) are collected after several daily injections of a growth factor. The growth factor stimulates the bone marrow to produce more stem cells and directs them from the bone marrow into the blood circulation, where they can be collected by a machine. Giving the growth factor and moving the cells into the blood stream is a process called "mobilization." Sometimes, the donor's bones may ache while receiving the growth factor. This pain will go away after the stem cells are collected and the patient is no longer receiving the growth factor. Collecting the stem cells on a machine is called "apheresis." Apheresis takes about three hours. The donor has an IV inserted into each arm so that the blood can circulate through a machine, where it is separated by centrifugal force into white blood cells, red blood cells, and platelets. The stem cells are in the white cell portion and are collected in a bag. The rest of the blood is returned to the donor. The donor may feel some tingling in his lips or fingertips from the anticoagulant that is in the IV fluid to keep the blood from clotting while circulating through the machine.

Umbilical cord blood is collected from the placenta and cord after a baby is born. A tissue-type test is done and recorded before the blood is frozen for future use by a patient who doesn't have a tissue-type matched donor.

Donors come in several forms. The most common donor is a sibling who has the same human leukocyte antigen (HLA) type. A transplant from another person is called an allogeneic transplant. An identical twin is the most perfectly matched donor. A transplant from an identical twin is referred to as syngeneic. If a patient doesn't have a matched brother or sister, a closely matched father, mother, cousin, or other relative may be the donor. This is known as a "mismatched" allogeneic transplant.

What does it feel like to be a bone marrow donor?

"It hurt." Tyler, age 8

"Being my sister's donor made me happy. I love my sister, and I wanted to help her. It was painful after I went through the process of them getting my bone marrow, but the pain didn't last that long. I was nervous." Tamisha's sister, age 12

"Jacob says he doesn't remember donating his bone marrow when he was almost two-and-a-half years old. He just kept asking, 'Why are we here?'" Anna, age 8

"As the donor and Cynthia's mother, it was a very scary, uncertain time in our lives. It was also very rewarding for me to see my daughter being given a new chance at life. I encourage everyone to sign up as a donor." Mother of a transplant recipient

An unrelated donor may be an option if the patient doesn't have a family member who can be a donor. The National Marrow Donor Program can try to match a patient with the thousands of people who have agreed to be a bone marrow donor. If a match is found, the donor goes to a designated hospital nearby for a complete examination. His marrow is harvested there, and a courier carries it to the center where the patient has been receiving treatment.

When Stevie was finished getting all the chemotherapy and radiation, it was time for Anna to give her stem cells to him. Her blood was exactly like Stevie's, so she was chosen to be his donor.

Anna's mom and dad went with her to the operating room. The doctor gave her medicine so that she would go to sleep and not feel anything. He then poked Anna's hip bones with a needle and syringe and sucked out the bone marrow. He put it into a clean plastic bag.

When Anna woke up, she felt some pain in her hips. The nurse gave her medicine to help her feel better. She didn't feel like playing for a few days, but soon she was feeling like herself again.

The last type of transplant is an autologous transplant. This is when patients are their own donors. Patients with solid tumors or in remission can have their bone marrow or PBSC collected, frozen, and stored until after chemotherapy and radiation. They then receive their own stem cells.

"The stem cell collections weren't scary at all. I lay in bed, looked up to the machine, played Nintendo, and watched TV. One time, as soon as they finished collecting cells, I got a bad stomachache. The nurses knew what to do and gave me medicine. My stomachache went right away. They said my stomachache was from the medicine they gave me after my stem cell collection to keep my blood from clotting, I think." Jarrett, age 5

A nother way to get stem cells is from the blood in your veins. The patient in the hospital room next to Stevie had an older sister, Jennifer, who was her donor. Jennifer got a special medicine called a "growth factor" for a few days that made her bone marrow make lots of stem cells. Then a nurse put an IV in each arm so the blood could go through a machine that collected her stem cells. This process is called apheresis.

Now that the chemotherapy and radiation therapy have killed all the cancer, it's time for the stem cells to do their work. The bone marrow or PBSC is brought to the patient's room, and tubing is attached to the central line. The cells are infused slowly at first, but if the patient tolerates them satisfactorily, they are infused a little more quickly. If the patient is getting his own frozen stem cells, the plastic bags are thawed in a warm water bath and infused through the central line.

The side effects of the infusion of the stem cells are usually minimal. Some patients may experience nausea, fever, or high blood pressure. Cells that have been frozen have a distinctive odor from a preservative called DMSO. The patient can taste it, and people in the room and hallway can smell it. The odor has been described in a variety of ways—from creamed corn to garlic.

"I thought that a bone marrow transplant would be a complex surgery, but it's about as simple as a regular blood transfusion." Kristine, age 16

It's day 0—Stevie's new birthday, even though he didn't feel like a party. It's the day he got his new bone marrow. The nurse gave him his new stem cells through his central line just like a blood transfusion.

The amazing part of the transplant happens as the cells migrate from the blood stream to the bone marrow. There, they find the factory and start making more blood cells. Watching the daily white blood cell count, especially the absolute neutrophil count (ANC)—also called poly count, granulocyte count, neutrophil count, or simply counts—is exciting as days 10-15 approach. This is when the first signs of "engraftment" take place. Engraftment is the process of the bone marrow making more blood cells. The time it takes for this to happen varies depending on what type of transplant the patient received—autologous, allogeneic, or unrelated donor—and whether it was bone marrow or PBSC.

S tevie tried to imagine that he was a drop of bone marrow. He wanted to find his way back to the factory so he could start making more blood. It sounded kind of hard, but it's the bone marrow's job. Anna put a calendar on the wall to mark off the days and write down his counts.

Keeping a patient occupied during recovery is a challenge. A balance must be maintained between keeping active and staying comfortable.

"My family helped me by being with me and playing games." Tyler, age 8

"They helped me think about good things. They helped me feel better and feel like this was normal." Jarrett, age 5

"Always treat them the same as you would. On their good days, play games. With my sister, we listened to our favorite radio station and played video games a lot." Tamisha, 18

"I drew pictures to decorate my dad's room. The patients are supposed to walk around their floor, so I made him a chart to monitor how many times he walked around each day." Emily, age 8, daughter of patient

"My mother stayed day and night with me. I love her very much and always felt safe when she was with me. She would hold my hand and dry my tears and tell me she loved me. Just knowing that she was there and that I didn't have to go through anything alone made me feel so safe and made me believe everything would be all right." Ethel, age 15

It was getting a little boring, so Stevie, his mom and dad, and Anna played games, worked on puzzles, and even did some school work. Walking in the hall or riding a bicycle helped Stevie to keep his muscles strong. He even made a "map" chart for each lap he walked or each minute on the bicycle—one square was a mile closer to home. When he wasn't feeling well, he watched a favorite video or someone read a book to him.

The first common side effect after transplant is mucositis, a sore mouth and throat. This occurs when there aren't enough white blood cells to kill the bacteria that are normally in the mouth. Keeping the mouth clean is one way to prevent a severe infection, but most patients require an IV narcotic to control the pain. The mouth pain starts to go away when the white blood cell count rises after the transplant.

Here's some advice on facing scary things from patients who know.

"Try to focus on happy thoughts of a family trip and ask questions because some things that seem scary at the time, when they are explained, it doesn't seem all that big of a deal. If something was painful, my doctor told me to take deep breaths and exhale slowly. I even used soothing music to take my mind off the pain." Tamisha, age 18

"Talk to someone." Karl, age 9, brother of patient

"Just remember to take everything a day at a time. Be aware of what might be the long-term outcome. Just take every day and what happens during that day separately, without forgetting what the big picture is." David, age 11

"Mommy and Daddy holding me kept me happy. I was told that I helped a patient's daddy feel better about the hospital and the possibility of recovery for his baby daughter by being happy and healthy and bouncing up and down the hospital halls full of life." Anna, age 8

"It's okay . . . it's gonna be okay." Elisabeth, age 5 (sister of patient)

W

hile Stevie was waiting to get better, he didn't feel very well. First, his throat and mouth got sore. Then, he didn't feel like eating. The nurse said it would help if he kept his mouth clean. He swished his mouth with water, and spit it out. The nurse gave him medicine in his central line to take away the pain.

Infections can be a serious complication after transplant, when the white blood cell count is low. Infections are caused by bacteria, fungi, or viruses. Prevention with prophylactic medications is important. Antibiotics are started when the white blood cell count dips below a certain level to prevent an infection when the patient has no resistance or immunity to these organisms. Acyclovir, ganciclovir, or other antiviral medications may be given to prevent herpes simplex virus or cytomegalovirus. Fluconazole may be given to prevent a fungal infection.

If the patient has a fever, blood cultures are taken to find the source of the infection so that the right antibiotic can be prescribed. Antibiotics fight infections caused by bacteria.

Some transplant units have special rooms called laminar air flow rooms. Everything in the room is sterile, even the air, which is filtered so that it is 99.7% germ-free. Everyone entering the room must wear a sterile gown, gloves, booties, head covering, and mask. The patient also can be accessed through a plastic curtain with plastic sleeves and gloves.

Everyone who has contact with the patient, from family to staff, can help to prevent infections by washing their hands. Effective hand washing entails scrubbing the hands with soap and warm water for at least 15 seconds. Hands should be washed before entering the patient's room, before and after eating, after using the toilet, and after nose blowing or sneezing. The patient, too, should be careful to wash his hands at these times and when he returns to his room after walking in the hall.

Germs can be a big problem after a transplant, so everyone who came into Stevie's room had to wash his hands first. He made a sign that said, "Sing 'Yankee Doodle Dandy' while you wash your hands." His nurse told him that's how long it takes to kill the germs.

A rising neutrophil count signals engraftment, when the graft—new cells from the donor—starts taking hold in the bone marrow. One problem that can occur at this time is graft versus host disease (GVHD). This is when the graft doesn't recognize its new home, the host. Because the host is like a foreign body, it tries to protect itself by fighting it. This reaction can affect the skin, gastrointestinal tract, or liver. The patient usually receives immunosuppressive drugs or steroids to keep the graft from "coming in too fast," giving the host a chance to get used to the new cells. The reaction may be as mild as a skin rash on the arms, diarrhea a couple of times daily, or a slight increase in the bilirubin. It could be as severe as a skin rash that resembles a third-degree burn, large volumes of bloody diarrhea, or liver failure. Doctors keep a close eye on these three symptoms and treat GVHD very carefully.

On Day 12, Stevie wrote down his counts on his calendar. "ANC is 350. Platelets are 25,000."

"Hey, everyone, my counts are going up!"

A couple of days later, the doctor told him that his ANC was more than 580 and that he didn't

need antibiotics or transfusions anymore. Yeah! Stevie's bone marrow factory was working again.

A couple of days after Stevie's counts started coming up, he got a skin rash on his stomach and arms. The little red pimples were itchy. The doctor said that Anna's stem cells needed time to get comfortable in their new home. The doctor gave Stevie medicine to help the new stem cells to get used to their new body and to help him feel better.

Patients sometimes have severe complications after transplant, including an overwhelming infection, GVHD, bleeding, or pneumonia. They may need special care in the intensive-care unit. Machines such as ventilators, cardiac monitors, kidney dialysis machines, or other monitoring devices may be necessary to care for some patients. This time period can be very frightening for the patient and family. Social workers, chaplains, and child-life specialists work closely with doctors and nurses to help everyone to get through this difficult time.

Family members usually are allowed to stay with the patient as much as possible but are asked to leave the room for some procedures. The patient is made as comfortable as possible with pain medication and tranquilizers. Sometimes patients seem like they are asleep, but they can still hear. Words of comfort and encouragement from loved ones are important at this time.

"We saw some patients die and saw their families grieving. We knew it could have happened to us, so life became more precious." Sarah, mother of patient

"Sometimes a friend dies, and it makes you really sad. You have to remember that they were really nice and helped you out a lot and be glad you had a chance to know them." Jarrett, age 5

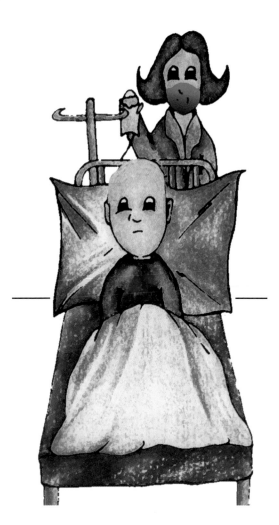

T he little boy in the room across the hall got really sick and had to go to the special room with lots of machines. He had his own nurse who took care of him all day. His doctors worked very hard to help him to get better.

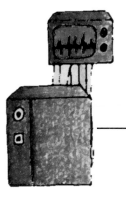

The day of discharge from the hospital is a milestone, although more recovery lies ahead. Requirements for discharge usually include an ANC of greater than 500 and a platelet count of greater than 20,000. The patient should be off IV antibiotics, antiemetics, and pain medication for one or two days and should be able to eat and drink enough that additional IV fluids are at a minimum. Caregivers should learn what symptoms to watch for—GVHD or other complications such as fever, rash, bleeding, change in mental status, and any acute pain—and when to report these symptoms to the doctor.

Routine visits to the clinic for blood tests, transfusions, and physical exams will fill the days for several weeks before it is time to go home. When blood tests are not needed as frequently and IV medications and transfusions are no longer needed, the central line can be removed.

"You know how it feels to have a stopped-up nose and then you blow and blow until it finally breaks loose and comes out? . . . Well, that's the great feeling you get when the Hickman comes out . . . relief!" Anna, age 8

F inally, was time for Stevie to get out of the hospital. He and his family stayed in the apartment near the hospital. He went to the clinic several times a week to see the doctors and nurses and to have blood tests done. It was fun to walk outside in the fresh air, but he didn't feel like running quite yet.

Going home is wonderful, but it also is difficult because others don't always understand what the patient and family have been through. They may think the experience is similar to recovering from an appendectomy or another course of regular chemotherapy. Here's what some people said about how they felt about going home.

"The night we arrived home, as we entered the city limits, about 200 people were gathered to greet us and welcome us home." Kristine, age 16

"We hated to leave the friends at the hospital we would never see again. We liked being together all the time. People at home weren't prepared to see Tyler because he had changed due to medications." Sarah, Tyler's mother

"My friends and family were standoffish when I got home. Everyone acted like I was made of glass and that if they talked to or touched me I'd shatter into a zillion pieces." Ethel, age 15

"I would say it took probably two years for life to get back to normal." Kristine, age 16

"For me, it took a year to get back into how I used to be before the transplant. I'm going to college and hanging out with friends again." Tamisha, age 18

O n Day 85, Stevie got to go home. Molly and Christopher and all his friends and neighbors were outside their house with a big red banner that said, "Welcome Home, Stevie!"

Stevie was glad to be home, even if he still didn't feel great. He still had to take his GVHD medicine, and food still didn't taste quite right.

Life was different than before his transplant. He had to be careful of germs and stay away from crowds. He didn't get to go back to school right away. Soon, however, he was feeling better, and the doctor said he could safely have fun the way he used to.

Suggested Reading

How it feels when a parent dies, Jill Krementz, Alfred A. Knopf, New York, 1981.

How it feels to fight for your life, Jill Krementz, Little, Brown, & Company, Boston, 1989.

My book for kids with cansur: A child's autobiography of hope, Jason Gaes, Melius and Peterson Publishing, Inc., Aberdeen, SD, 1987.

Bone marrow transplants: A guide for cancer patients and their families, Marianne L. Shaffer, Taylor Publishing, Dallas, 1994.

Bone marrow transplants: A book of basics for patients, Susan K. Stewart, BMT Newsletter, Highland Park, IL, 1995.

I want to grow hair, I want to grow up, I want to go to Boise, Erma Bombeck, Harper & Row, New York, 1989.

One small sparrow, Jeff Leeland, Multnomah Press, Sisters, OR, 1995.

Survivor: Taking control of your fight against cancer, Laura Landro, Simon & Schuster, New York, 1998.